Captain Noah and His Floating Zoo

by Michael Flanders & Joseph Horovitz

Cantata in popular style arranged for male lead and
SATB, with piano, optional bass and drums

Novello Publishing Limited

NOV200156

PREFACE

We chose Noah as our subject because it offered such a splendid, dramatic shape for setting to music as a group of songs. If you look it up, you will see that our version follows the Old Testament story very closely (when we did, we were surprised to find we had forgotten all about the Raven and the domestication of animals!). The work is not intended as a contribution to 'pop' religion. We hope it will be useful wherever and whenever groups of singers and musicians need a work of some length to perform together, and that they will arrange, divide and adapt it (within reason) as best suits their available talent and the occasion. It has been designed as a choral, rather than a theatrical, piece; but various semi-dramatic effects or stagings may suggest themselves.

The work can be performed with piano accompaniment alone, but a separate part each for string bass and jazz drums is available on hire. Guitar may be added, playing from the score. Various optional percussion instruments may be used here and there for special effects, such as at the start (thunder) and in No. 3 where maracas, claves and tambourines may help to accentuate the Latin-American flavour of the Samba.

Finally, we strongly recommend our metronome markings, and we do feel that the piece should be performed as a continuous whole, with the shortest possible breaks between each number.

Michael Flanders & Joseph Horovitz

The original version of this cantata, for unison or two-part voices & piano, is also available in vocal score.

DURATION ABOUT 26 MINUTES

Cover design by Harold King

CAPTAIN NOAH AND HIS FLOATING ZOO

Cantata in popular style arranged for male lead and SATB, with piano, optional bass and drums

by

MICHAEL FLANDERS and JOSEPH HOROVITZ

INTRODUCTION

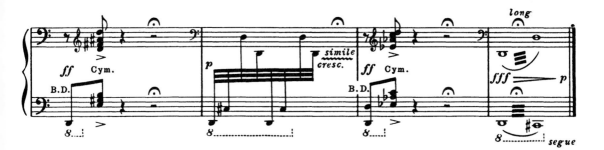

No. 1

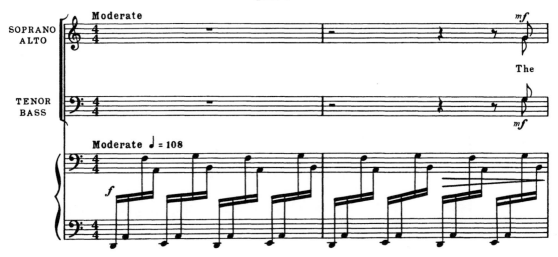

20014

SOLO *mf*

'It

Lord looked down on the earth and it made him sad.

should have been good what I made but it turned out bad.

There's

no-thing but sin-ning, wick-ed-ness and vi-o-lence there!

Re-

4

wash those sin-ners down the drain!

Rain and rain and rain and rain and

rain! But

No - ah and his fam-i - ly they've been good.

Go,

6

(SOLO) 3

No-ah, build me an ark, of go-pher wood; make it four - fif-ty long, by se-ven-ty-five feet wide, and three decks tall, with a roof and a door in the side, ___ 'cos I'm gon-na make it

S
A
T rain and rain and rain and rain and
B

A7 Dm6 Em7 Dm6 A9+5

20014

When the ark is fin-ished, here is what you have to rain!

Dm6 Em7-5 Dm A7 Dm6 Em7 Dm6 A9+5

mf

(SOLO)

do:— You fill it with a-ni-mals, *yes, with* a-ni-mals two by

Dm6 Em7-5 Dm A7 Dm6 Em7 Dm6 A9

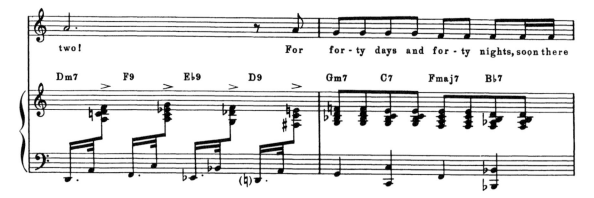

two! For for-ty days and for-ty nights, soon there

Dm7 F9 E♭9 D9 Gm7 C7 Fmaj7 B♭7

(♮)

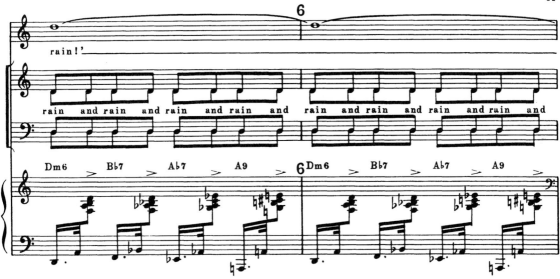

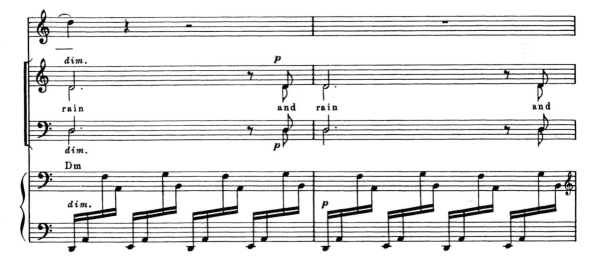

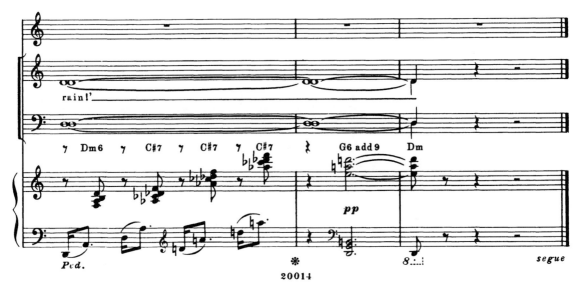

No. 2

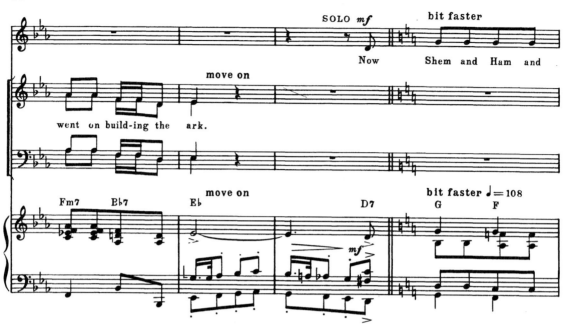

SOLO *mf*   bit faster

Now Shem and Ham and

move on

went on build-ing the ark.

move on   bit faster ♩=108

Fm7   Bb7   Eb   D7   G   F

9

Ja-phet, they were the sons of Noah. He made them get all kinds of food and

G   F   G   F   G   C G   F   G   F

(SOLO)

lay them in a store; said Mis-sis Noah:

1 SOPRANO (from CHORUS) *mf*

'Ten - thou-sand buns, what

G   F   G   C   G   C7   F   D7-9

'E-do we need them for? E-nough to feed an E-le-phant!'

Gm Eb9 D7+5 G9 C9 Fmaj9 Bbmaj7 Eb9

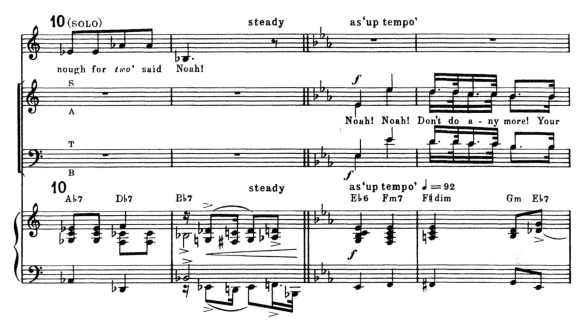

10 (SOLO) steady as 'up tempo'

nough for *two*' said Noah!

Noah! Noah! Don't do a-ny more! Your

10 steady as 'up tempo' ♩=92

Ab7 Db7 Bb7 Eb6 Fm7 F#dim Gm Eb7

boat's a laugh-ing-stock! Ha! Ha! But Noah went right on build-ing the ark, and his

Ab 7 C7 Fm Bb7 Eb6 Eb7 Ab Gm C7

move on

ham-mer went knock, knock, knock! No - ah's ham-mer went knock, knock, knock!

move on

11

Fm Bb7 Eb Db7-5 C7 Fm7 Bb7 Eb

SOLO *mf* bit faster ♩=108

Then Noah told his sons to do all

Bbm Eb B7 E D E D

12

that the Lord had planned, to fetch him ev-'ry kind of thing that's

E D E A E D E D

liv-ing on dry land; the ones you see down on the farm, the

E D E A Dm7 G C7 F D7-9

ones you see in zoos, all rep-tiles, birds and in-sects too, and line them up in

Gm　Eb9　D7+5　G9　C9　Fmaj9　Bbmaj7　Eb9　Ab7　Db7

sf

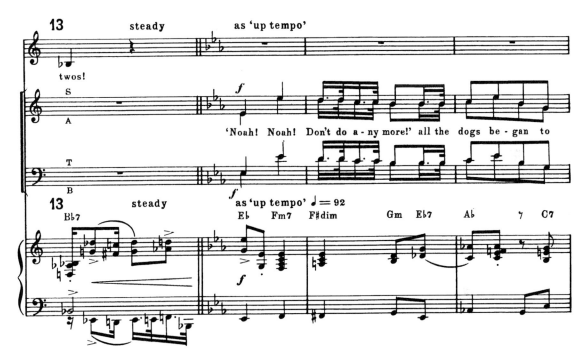

13 steady as 'up tempo'

twos!

S

A

f

'Noah! Noah! Don't do a-ny more!' all the dogs be-gan to

T

B

13 steady as 'up tempo' ♩ = 92

Bb7　　Eb　Fm7　F#dim　Gm　Eb7　Ab　7　C7

f

mf

bark, 'Just hark at him, old Jun-gle Jim!' But he went on build-ing the

1 TENOR ALL

mf

Fm　　Bb7　Eb6　Eb7　Ab　Gm　C7　Fm　Bb7

sf *mf*

14

ark, No-ah! went on build-ing, and he went on build-ing, and he went on build-ing the

Eb Db7 C7 Fm7 Bb7 Bbm6 C7 Fm7 Bb7
-5

ark! _____

Eb6 Fm7 F#dim Gm Eb7 Ab Db7 F#7 Bb7 Eb

segue

No. 3

Samba ♩=104
Ab7 B7 Ab7 B7 **15** E9 Gmaj7-5 E9 Gmaj7-5

pp

tenderly, but same tempo   **16**   SOLO *p*

Then

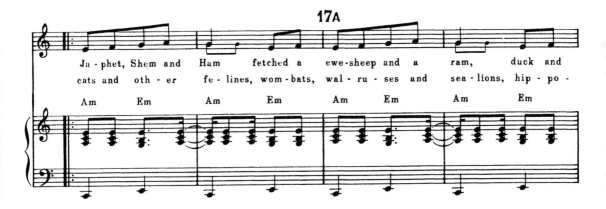

17A

Ja - phet, Shem and Ham   fetched a   ewe-sheep and a   ram,   duck and
cats and oth - er   fe - lines, wom-bats, wal - ru - ses and   sea - lions, hip - po -

drake and bull and   cow and cock and hen,   male and
po - ta - mi and   spi - ders and g - nus,   bears and

17

fe-male spot-ted chee-tahs, ar-ma-dil-los and ant-eat-ers and mos-
bees and gold-en eag-les, hor-ses, har-vest-mice and sea-gulls, apes and

17B

qui-*ters* and two li-ons from their den. All the
hum-ming-birds and worms and kan-ga- roos.

All mar-su-pi-als and mam-mals, such as

18

wal-la-bies and cam-els, snakes and cen-ti-pedes, a pair of ev-'ry one;

they got stuck with one gir - affe, till they found his bet - ter

19

half, then from an - te - lope to ze - bra, it was done! Yes,

ev - 'ry liv - ing crea - ture that walks up - on this earth or_ creeps up - on its

20

bel - ly on the land, or_ flies up in the air, just you

name it, it was there; it's one pair of each, just as the Lord had planned.

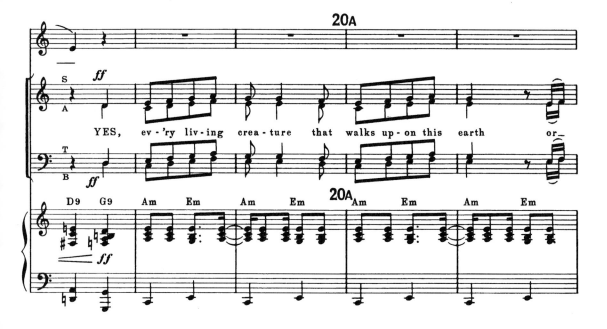

20A

YES, ev-'ry liv-ing crea-ture that walks up-on this earth or

land, creeps up-on its bel-ly on the land, _____ or flies up in the

air, just you name it, it was there; it's one pair of each, just as the Lord had

20B

Dm7 G7 Em Am7 Em7-5 A7 Dm Dm7 G7

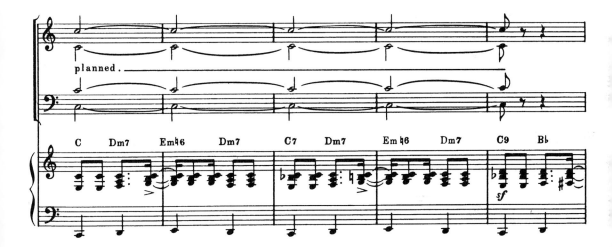

planned.

C Dm7 Em♮6 Dm7 C7 Dm7 Em♮6 Dm7 C9 B♭

'Noah! Noah! Don't do an-y more!' said the

B♭+5 C9 F Am Dm Am7 **21** Dm6 G9 Am7 Em

peo - ple, 'what a lark!' As crea - tures

came by ev - 'ry name, and he led them in-to the ark, No-ah!

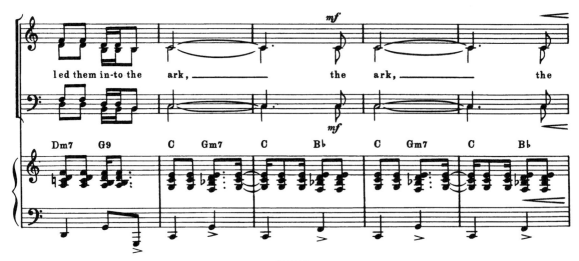

led them in-to the ark, _____ the ark, _____ the

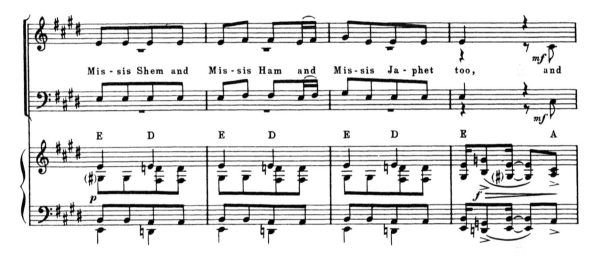

26

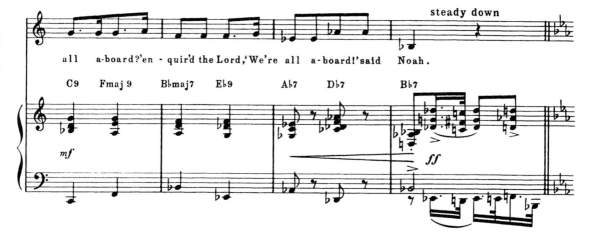

20014

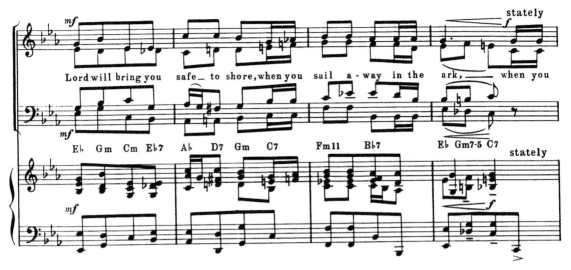

No. 4

It looks like rain, now won't that just be jol-ly!__ It

29

looks like rain, you know, I thought it would! It

looks like rain, I must go and get my brol-ly; a short, sharp show-er will

do the flow-ers good!

It looks like rain—

20014

in fact, it's real-ly pour-ing, it looks like

rain! The ground has turned to mud! It

looks like rain! Can you hear the riv-er roar-ing? I

should-n't be sur-prised___ if it was going to flood!

And

now it's round my ank-les, and now it's round my knees; and

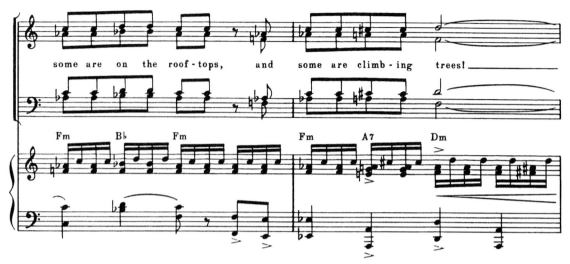

some are on the roof-tops, and some are climb-ing trees!

Oh God for-give me

please! Oh God for - give me

31

please!   It   looks   like   the   sea   is

Bm   (Bm6)   Bm   (Bm6)   Dm   G   Dm

shout

ri - sing like a foun - tain; it   looks   like...   HELP!   I'm

Dm   Dm   Fm   Abm

shout

shout

mak - ing   for   the   moun - tain, it   looks   like...   AHH!   The

Abm   Em   Gm

shout

34

The wa-ter's round my shoul-ders and I'm Glug! Glug!

world's a brim-ming jug!

(SOLO) slower ♩ = 84

Glug!

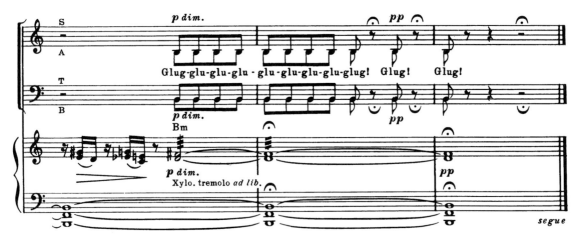

Glug-glu-glu-glu - glu-glu-glu-glu-glug! Glug! Glug!

Xylo. tremolo *ad lib.*

segue

No. 5

35
somewhat more swaying

Then all things liv-ing and breath-ing___ on the face of the

earth did drown; ___ for ev-en the peaks of the moun -

tains were a good five___ fath-oms___ down, way down, a good five___

38

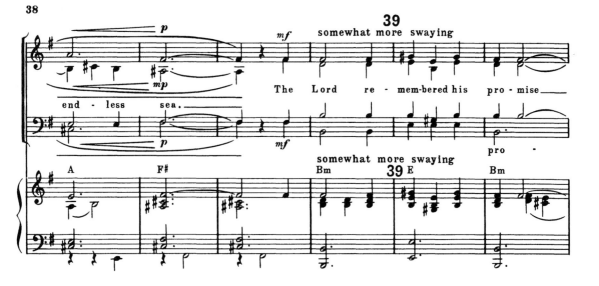

20014

No.6

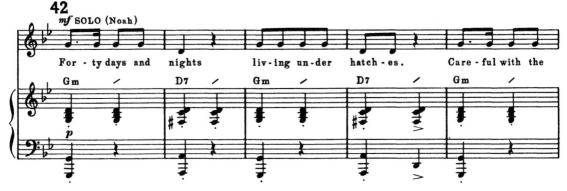

wait-ing to be fed. For the rain's stead-y drum-ming on the roof a-bove my

head, the rain-drops drum-ming o-ver-head!

Here in-side the ark,

rol-ling, pitch-ing, turn-ing, ev-'ry-thing is dark, no more oil for

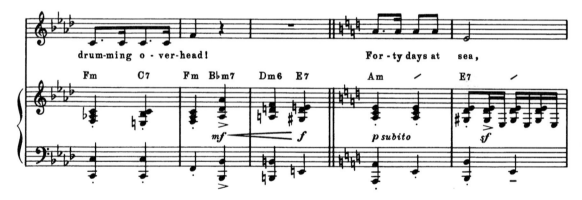

rud-der, but I hope he won't hear when I wish that I were dead! With the

rain's stead-y drum-ming on the roof a-bove my head, the rain-drops

move on gradually

drum-ming o - ver-head!

slightly faster *about* ♩ = 100

Comes a-noth-er day

dif - f'rent from the oth-ers: Shem be-gins to say some-thing to his

broth-ers— but his voice stops short! There's noth-ing to be said... The rain is-n't

drum-ing on the roof a-bove my head! The rain's stopped drum-ming o-ver-

head! The rain's stopped drum-ming o-ver-head!

rain's stopped drum-ming o-ver-head! drum-ming o-ver-head!

No. 7

The ark went peace-ful-ly float - ing___ and the sea was

calm and flat_____ till the Lord God brought it to rest at

last, on the top of Mount A - ra - rat,_____ on top of Mount

last, on top

No. 8

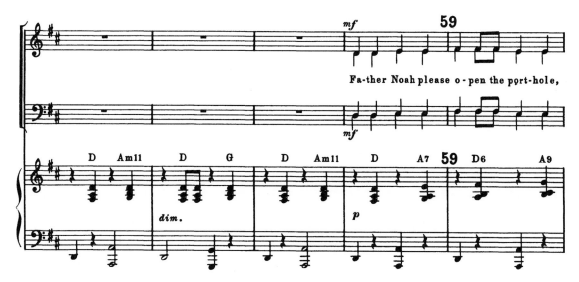

let's have a peep at the world out-side; though we thank the Lord who saved us—

optional shout

Cain and A - bel! What a ride! Can't be - lieve the ark's not mo - ving,

1 TENOR

optional shout

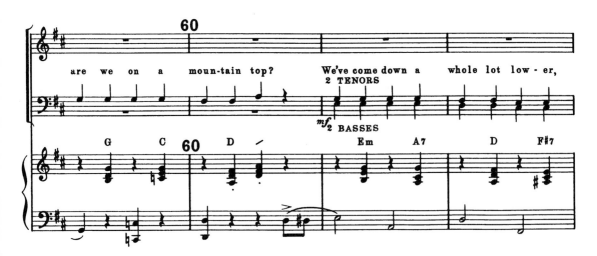

60

are we on a moun-tain top? We've come down a whole lot low - er,

2 TENORS

2 BASSES

60

I just felt my ears go pop! Let's have a peep through the port-hole, Fa-ther!
ALL

Mis-sis Shem is so ve-ry ti-ny

Mo-ther first! Then me! Then me!

she can't e-ven see the sea!

62

Fa-ther Noah sent forth a ra-ven, flapped a-round and shou-ted 'CAW!'

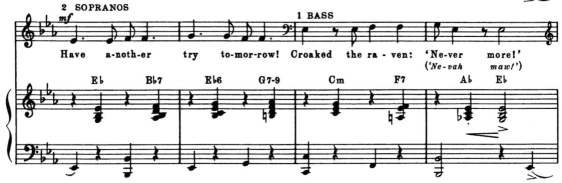

Have a-noth-er try to-mor-row! Croaked the ra-ven: 'Ne-ver more!'
('Ne-vah mawt!')

63

I can see our ti-ny is-land, is it real-ly A-ra-rat?

Let me lean out e-ven fur-ther... There goes Mis-sis Ja-phet's hat!

Let's have a peep through the port-hole, Fa-ther! Mis-sis Ham must have a shot!

So you boys can see my bloo-mers? Thank you, No! I'd ra-ther not!

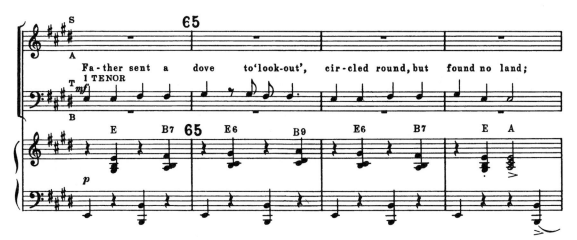

Fa-ther sent a dove to 'look-out', cir-cled round, but found no land;

then it flew right back through the port-hole, set-tled safe on Fa-ther's hand.

E   B7   E6   G#7-9   C#m   F#7   A   E

1 SOPRANO

mf

66

Sent the dove a - gain a - fly - ing af - ter wai - ting for a week;

A   D   E   A   D   66   E

mf

back it came, that ve - ry same ev'-ning, an o - live twig held in its beak.

F#m   B7   E   G#7   C#m   F#7   B7

sent the oth - er dove to join it; nei - ther one came back a - gain!

Now they need no ark for shel - ter, there the doves will build their nest—

where the o - live trees are grow - ing make their home and take their rest._

56

No. 9

more. Come out with your wife and your sons and daugh-ters

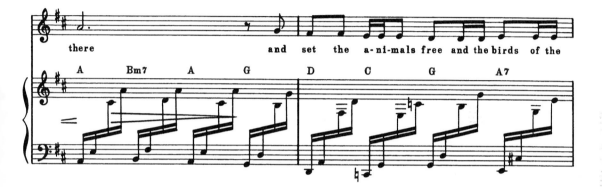

there and set the a-ni-mals free and the birds of the

air,' and they came out two by two by two by two by

two; two by two by two by two by two. The

segue

No. 10

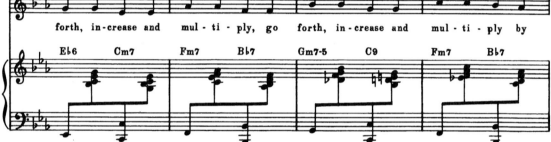

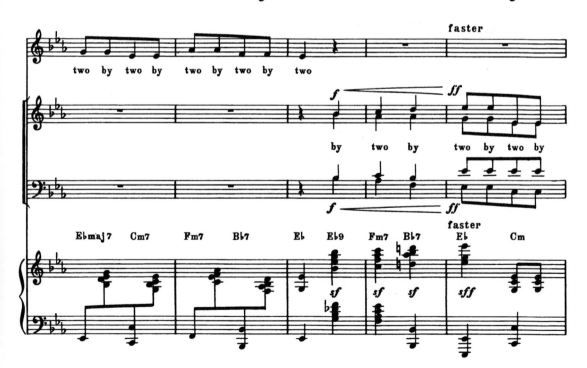

68

20014

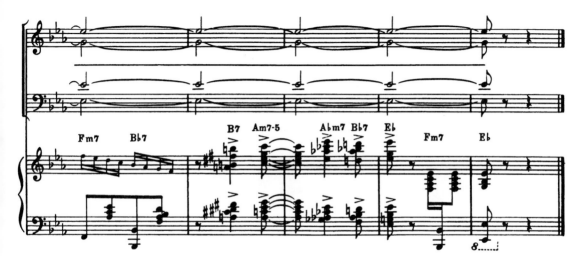

THE NOVELLO BOOK OF CAROLS

Compiled and Edited by
William Llewellyn

This major issue of 90 carols offers a balanced mixture of accompanied and unaccompanied items, most for mixed vooices, which are aptly suited to today's choral needs.

Contents include carols by:

Benjamin Britten	Kenneth Leighton
Richard Rodney Bennett	William Llewellyn
Ronald Corp	Philip Moore
Michael Head	Philip Radcliffe
Ian Humphris	Judith Weir
John Joubert	Robin Wells

From Giovanni Gabrieli to Judith Weir, medieval melodies to spirituals, the range of styles in The Novello Book of Carols encompasses a wide spectrum of tastes. Fresh arrangements of carols central to Christmas are set beside original compositions, and some fine medieval words contrast with new contemporary texts.

PLUS

■ fully comprehensive index
■ instructive performing notes
■ carols for the complete service or concert
■ exceptionally clear layout
■ 21 carols for school use,
published in The Novello Junior Book of Carols
■ alternative accompaniments available
in The Novello Brass Band Book of Carols

Novello